THE LABYRINTH OF MY LIFE

THE LABYRINTH OF MY LIFE…

ARCHITA RANI DASH

Woven Words Publishers OPC Pvt. Ltd.

Registered Office:

Vill: Raipur, P.O: Raipur Paschimbar,

Dist: Purba Midnapore, Pin: 721401,

West Bengal, India.

www.wovenwordspublishers.com

Email: editor@wovenwordspublishers.com

First published by Woven Words Publishers OPC Pvt. Ltd., 2018

Copyright© Archita Rani Dash, 2018

POETRY

IMPRINT: WOVEN WORDS FIRE

ISBN 13: 978-93-86897-31-2

ISBN 10: 9386897318

Price: $6

Printed and bound in India

For my beloved parents, my dearest elder sister **Amrita** *who always believed in me, my teachers and my loved ones who always encouraged and supported me.*

CONTENTS:

'Cause Some Things Are Never Meant To Be...

You know, some things never change!

Like the morning's cascading glory;
glory paving the way for the over powering scintillating
darkness.

Like me lost in your memories;
memories so insufficient that you still give me more memories
to be lost in.

Like my writings still somewhere in search of you;
you, somewhere lost in my words so difficult for me to
introspect.

You know, some things never happen!

The way a horizon is all but a deceiving skyline at infinity;
infinity giving vain hopes of the Earth kissing the sky.

The way I just only wished for a glimpse of the moonlight;
moonlight that gave me the whole damn dark sky along with it.

The way we make love to each other, each of us being at two
different Earth poles;
Earth poles which are too far enough to separate us forever.

Well, that is how some things are never meant to be.

Precipitates Of Their Last Love

Swayed away by the way
the Earth had united them,
not a single day in their lives had gone
by not waking up next to each other.

From sharing their good morning tea and snacks
at their favorite hangout joints
to exchanging their love with each other
over the finest genres of their musical tunes,
they both once relished every moment together.

Hand in hand they celebrated together
each other's every triumph every failure,
not a single festival or event of one
was celebrated ever with the absence of the other.

While she lend her ears to his *Azaan*,
he anticipated the *Pujas* which followed her entire day.
There once used to be this time when they boasted
of their intimate love and relationship
that nobody ever shared.

But this *oh-so-happy-go* love story
could not last long
'cause unlike many other tales of love
this had had lots of villains to flung.

With some self-created misunderstandings,
rumors and hatred between them,
the idea of their partition
finally struck the minds of those villains.

The love birds once *used-to-be-together*,
who never ever had thought of their separation,
then stood partitioned with much bloodshed
as *Hindustan* and *Pakistan*,
demarcated by the *Radcliffe Line!*

<u>Could You Come O'er To Me For A Night?</u>

Come over to me tonight.
Let us paint the dark sky, blue and bright.
Just like the very first day, do you still remember?
When our eyes didn't meet each other?
All we did was only fumble.

How I wish!
All those very initial days of love we could again cherish.
Too nervous to say anything;
All the more shy to even stare.

Now that all this far we have come together.
In love, fights, pampering, trust, understanding and laughter
Growing so stronger together.

Could you please come over to me just for a night?
Only to paint the dark sky, blue and bright;
Taking both of us back to the day of our very first sight!

The Cheapest Thrills

Standing here to unveil the cheapest of the thrills,

not a word of mine would lie to you,

for I've always tasted my nation's salt

and so, it's my utmost responsibility for my nation's truth to be revealed.

The very first moment her cries as an infant were heard,

her parents sighed for they already knew her traditionally planned fate;

while the society got delighted for
yet another upcoming party was knocking at its gate!

Deprived of all sorts of unnecessary tensions
and burdens like education, examination and employment,

they just simply ensured her to enjoy her illiterate comfort by sitting at home,

and to gradually contribute towards social service by expertizing in all sorts of household chores for all.

When she finally attains the age of eight or ten,

it's now time for her to seek the pleasure of pain,

and then the cheapest journey full of the cheapest thrills begins.

She is offered to marry an adolescent boy elder to her;

this on denying or delaying leaves her with no other option
other than to marry an old aged man sometimes even a
divorcee or a widower.

So, what? At least as per my nation's most decorated traditional
norms,

she's getting married to someone

who would ultimately end up treating her like no one.

Immediately after she attains her puberty,

she is privileged with the responsibility
of mothering many kids risking her own immunity.

She is in fact fortunate enough to have such parents
taking so much pride for having gotten her a groom.

The society too rejoices in this ceremonial affair
in order to hide its evil ugly face.

Alas! For no one ever bothered

all those sleepless days and nights when her soul cried,

yet in the imposed process of having the cheapest thrills in her
life,
at a very young age she finally died!

Where Do I Make My Stand?

Tried and tested by the heart and the mind,
I still struggle midway,
like a beginner funambulist
cautious enough not to make my senses go blind,
to find where do I stand.

For all the crisscrossed ways
that I have travelled all alone so far,
and for all those unknown untrodden ways
yet to be travelled to go the farthest,
I fear not the mockery I've faced by all others.

In the art of funambulism,
what if I lose my balance and
fail to make my stand is what I fear!
'Cause ultimately I don't want to live
a life full of regrets;

Regrets for not having loved someone
with a broken heart at least for once;
regrets for not having been through snares and temptations
so as to learn to overcome them;
regrets for not having opted for
the unchosen choices for once,
regrets for having travelled through a commoner's path
instead of a funambulist's path!

For it is then only
I believe I'll carve out my way for myself;

I am going to make my stand one day,
so far away and high enough a place
for anyone to even wonder.

The Smell Of My Backyard

If my backyard would smell of anything,
it would be

of those long lost fresh love
still alive lingering in search of
you in the form of dew drops,
with those dew drops kissing the grasses
in remembrance of your body parts;

of those wayward withered dandelions
still hovering around in wait of
your single sensual kiss
to set them free in the air.

The Deceiving Dream!

Tormented by the mundane reality,
I asked my dream one night
if he really existed
and had come to me just for my sake?

Without even giving a second thought,
he nodded his head
and said, "Anything for you my darling",
with a heavenly smile on his pink luscious lips.

I asked him, "What makes you stay so far away?
For my heart always longs for your presence
throughout the day yet you bother to come to me
only when the night casts its sleepy spells on me!"

He then told me,
"Day time is too rush an hour for me
to spend my complete time with you;
Night is the time when I prefer
to see and know all of you."

By that time, his eyes were close to mine,
his nose touching the edge of my nose
yet his tempting lips still didn't
bother to implant kisses on mine.

He further continued,
"Morning accompanies the indubitable reality
that makes it impossible for anyone to believe me;

make it pretty easy for me to anyone into my trance."

I still questioned him,
"If, unlike the harsh reality,
you are a pleasant, beloved dream
then why do you need a specific hour to meet
someone so as to make her believe your surrealism?"

His eyes then lost its contact with mine,
the sounds of his heavy breathing started to fade away,
I found him scuffling towards a small locked door next to my
bed
whose keys have I never had seen.

The more I yearned for him,
the more he was found hurrying towards that door;
and the moment he appeared before the door,
its gates got wide opened as if those were waiting
for the loud thumping of every step he made.

And just as when he was about to step out of my room,
He uttered with a sigh, "I hail from a parallel universe
whose existence is exactly known by none;
I am no playboy but
yes, I do have to attend someone else's call."

He still continued, "Don't ever think that I've betrayed you
for I always justified the time we both were allotted
to know each other, to get close to each other;
You and I are simply inseparable."

"The more you question my existence
the more you shall lose yourself in a void space;
but the more you chase after me
the more you shall find me in you;
for I am that inevitable, eternal
beloved of yours and of many;
I am that never-ending *Deceiving Dream* of all!"

With this he vanished to the
void space of his parallel universe,
to which my eyes opened to welcome the sunshine
while still awaiting desperately to date my dream again at night!

My Kind Of Love Dates Be Like....

Do hell with the romanticising lunch or dinner dates!

Take me on bullet ride,
let my heart beat in sync with its 'Dug-Dug' sound.

Take me to an Old School Library,
let me be lost in its fantasizing world of books.
Ahh! Their smell be like I can die for...

Take me on a long walk by the beach side.
Let the waves do the talk to me
and let the sun kiss me hard until I get tanned.

Damn your bottles of unconsciousness
whose taste you don't even relish when you're drunk!
Take me to an antique Coffee shop and let me be in trance with
its aroma
and savour its every single sip of
strong blend of coffee to the fullest.

Take me to an uninhabited offbeat place.
Let's gig together with our guitars echoing amidst the
wilderness
and let the nature sing us a song.

Now that you wished to date me,
tell me can you make this "Old School- Wanderlust Love" date
to me?

My Roses In The Desert

I planted my roses in the desert
to let it bloom all alone
in the arid land
with all my effort.

Many planters offered me their lands
painted with petals of
blue, yellow, orange and red
with themselves bragging the magic in their hands.

I denied their tempting offers
and then they threw laughter and glances of mockery at me
considering me a madwoman
who never believed roses grow not on lands which lacked
waters.

I was too determined to give up
on planting those roses in the small piece of desert
that my life had gifted me out of the blue
for like their master, my roses too weren't that easy enough to
give up.

I truly believed miracles can happen through anyone's hand
it only takes to have the right faith, confidence and patience
for then one morning I found my roses painting the desert
with scarlet and lavender blooming on the barren land.

The World Has Ended!

The world has ended
Like it never had a beginning before.

Crisscrossed with the broken emotions
Defiled with the vilest nature.

Strangling to death everything that once bloomed
The horrid hearts causing you to swoon.

No peace no freedom
Even when it had a life.

Troubled hearts troubled minds
Making troubled inventions to not last for a lifetime.

The world has finally ended
Like it never meant to have had a beginning before.

But Like You said Mumma!

But like you said Mumma,
life is all about this tortuous road,
leading and misleading all this while,
masking and unmasking so many we pass by,
full of trusts yet betrayals nevertheless,
acts of hugging and kissing,
also the acts of back stabbing and smothering;
yet to keep fighting for the existence of one own self.

But my dear Mumma, why didn't you tell me,
while exhibiting all these fair and unfair plays of the life,
we even lose own identity, value of our own selves?
Did you really forget to tell
Or you actually hate to disclose the reality of the other side of
this unnerving tale?

But like you said Mumma,
our words are all that define us,
building and breaking ourselves,
hurting and comforting so many,
encouraging and discouraging other souls,
poisoning and remedying the minds of every listener;
yet to keep maintaining a control on the words that we utter.

But my dear Mumma, why didn't you tell me,
while handling our words with care,
the very words also play a wise game with us;
there come these promises and the trust we put in those words,
just to remind us that they exist only in broken forms
and by the time they leave us,
they ensure we are no more left as whole beings but mere
broken pieces.
Did you really forget to tell

through?

And now after all that you've said Mumma,
How I wish I could be just like you!

The Ballad Of Lost Souls

Somewhere deep down in the earth
buried are the strong desires;
desires to love more,
desires to live more.

Their screams could no longer be heard
nor their bodies could be recovered;
recovered to live a life of no regrets,
recovered to live their dreams.

Some took their lives for granted
while seeking the worldly lusts and pleasures;
pleasures to distract their minds from the death call,
pleasures to mask their coward souls.

Whereas others lived a life condemned
cursed and detested by themselves;
with themselves unsatisfied of the gifted life,
with themselves in dire want of more and more.

Amidst all these, they prioritized
satisfying their undying desires,
in pleasing other beings,
striving for the possessions
that didn't even bother to shed a tear when their souls were
lost.

Alas! For they did all but
only to love their living souls;
living souls that breathed just for their own sake,
souls that are perhaps no more alive,
those lost souls whose musings are engraved

I Am Your Poem

I am the poem
that you feel between your fingers
intertwined with that of your lover's.

I am the poem
which comes uninvited and
flows with the flow of unsaid words.

I am the poem
which rains over you
even when your life's a drought.

I am the poem
who believes in rolling down your eyes
when you believe you're rendered emotionless.

I am the poem
that becomes your prayers to the Almighty
even when you still remain an atheist.

I am the poem
who becomes the silhouette
of your darkness.

I am the poem
just meant only for you
and all about you!

<u>The Mirror On The Wall</u>

Every time I run to you,
you flatter me up by showing me
only the most beautiful side of mine,
saying me that the sunflowers bloom
only to the sunshine.

I have heard you saying the same
to whosoever runs to you
as if to hide the prickliness of a cactus
by making them bear the cactus-flowers.

I wonder how can you
show one to oneself
when you can't even see your real self?
Are you the truth revealing mirror
or are you the devil's watch to hover on the wall?

What spell did you cast on her
that she had to break his heart
with her winged eye-liner,
blood red lips and mascara put on?

And yet when he came running
all the way back to you,
you had nothing to do but
only to flatter him again
by saying it's time then
to find someone new again?

The Labyrinth of My Life | Archita

How I wish you were only
a true reflective piece!
Without you having to deceive one
of one's own appearance,
without you having to break someone
else's heart for having trusted
on the one who had the trust on you.

Now when I look at you,
I do hardly trust you,
for your fanciful appearance
to me makes no more sense!

Still stuck on the wall,
every time I run to you,
you continue to flatter me yet again;
though I know the sunflowers won't bloom now
for now there's no sunshine in my life;
yet I love the way you show me the flattery reflection,
the only thing that I can trust on,
for I too was once heartbroken.

Beauty And The Grave

What makes you take so much pride
in your beauty?
Your beauty which is as decorative
as the graveyard!

Graveyard which flaunts its external beauty
with clean, neatly labelled gravestones;
Gravestones which reflect only
their external fanciful beauty.

Beauty which hides
innumerable decayed flesh and bones
underneath the graves
that is never seen nor bothered by anyone.

Beauty with which you judged
whom to love and whom not;
beauty that made you self-obsessed
to such an extent that
what it is to love you knew not.

Graves that reflect your pride in your beauty in a similar way...

The Monopoly Of The Waves

Living by the shores of the ocean,
I was eroded away by the waves.
Drifting amidst the waters of the ocean,
I was somewhere abandoned at the shore all withered.

I questioned to myself,
"Where is the safest fate meant to be?"

Desperately seeking my answers in the eroding waves of the
ocean,
In the fading light of the horizon,
Chilling breeze of the land;
Hardly did I realise
There were few words left unsaid and few unheard.

For everyone's a prisoner in this sinister world,
A prisoner of their own words;
Few words which enjoy their right to freedom while
Others get chained down behind the bars.

Rest are believed to have died a premature death
For there never has been nor will there ever be
any safest place for the safest fate to reside in.

Mirage

To your existence,
one could never question;
to your vanishing lines of hope,
one could never doubt.
You come and go
as a beautiful hallucination
too difficult for anyone to behold.

Your beginning and your ending
knows no bounds;
you are quite an artist
who excels in pleasing every soul.
You make sure
your show goes well attended
without any expectations and disappointments.

At least you come to feed
with your fantasizing hopes
when there's no hope.
At least your surrealism
satisfies a soul from a distance
when everything else is all broke.

Oh you *Mirage*, the mother of the *Chimera*!
I plead your fire breath to consume away
the sins and chaos of this world;
making their existence
as your mere blurred imagery
only to be traced as

The Torn Gray Clouds

The clouds above me tore one fine day.
They started raining over me.
I began to stitch them one by one.

By the time I stitched the first cloud
and went on stitching the second,
waters started dripping again from the first.
The same continued to happen when I moved
from the second to the third and so on.

I rushed to the stationary shop in want of new threads
to sew the clouds very strong.
The shopkeeper gave me some
saying that those would hardly last long.
I grabbed them in no time considering them
to be manageable for the time being.

By the time I came back,
I found each of the clouds were on the verge of
breaking into pieces and pouring down rain incessantly.
I started sewing as fast as I could
with as many multiple stitches as I could.

Ultimately, the gray clouds broke into pieces.
Pieces which couldn't be collected to be stitched together.
I realized it was too late.
Too late for the town clouds to be stitched and for me to stitch
them.

<u>Forever Is Just A Myth</u>

I have seen
words receding from the promises made,
emotions receding from the moments cherished,
past thoughts backing off from the future plans,
the hearts backing off from establishing soulful connections.

I have known
rumors proving out to be the truth in no time,
close ones proving out to be the backstabbers,
goodbyes leaving the worst of the memories behind,
the loved ones smiling from a distant star leaving their bodies
behind.

I have realized
the lazy Sundays signaling the start of detestable busy Mondays,
maintaining a calorie controlled diet fills the heart with
remorse,
the perfect curves in a body does never really exist,
societal norms and stereotypes are just meant to be broken
after all no matter what you are going to judged anyway.

Yeah, I have myself witnessed
"forever is just a myth" and nothing else!

<u>Until We Meet The Next Time...</u>

Drained out of all energy
my body could no longer
sustain the long wait for my train,
delayed for the past 6 hours
and for another 4 hours to come.

Having nothing to do
on the small isolated platform
of a small town,
my eyes were in constant desperate search
to get hold of the sight
of a book shop.

Disappointed with my unsuccessful results,
I better thought to grab a soda bottle
from an old seller man
to beat the tiredness and my body heat
'cause of the entire afternoon's long wait.

Excluding me, of all the 5 passengers
who had waited at the platform along with me,
by then were all lucky enough
to have their onboard experiences
during the first 5 hours of my waiting.

Frustrated, exhausted and helpless,
sat down I on a small bench
at the 8th hour of the night;
praying God for his miracles to happen

Just a few minutes later,
I noticed a tall, dark guy
with a striking muscular figure
was sitting on the bench next to mine;
I wondered at his very sight
if he was the savior in disguise
that the God had sent for me!

Anyway, I checked my mobile's screen
to know the time left for my waiting
and then excited at the thought of
just having to wait for another 30 minutes,
I plugged in my earphones and
played the music.

It was then when I noticed
a huge shadow on the floor
just next to my travel bag.
I looked up immediately to find
the same tall, dark, handsome guy
standing next to me,
offering me a book in his hand.

That very moment did I realize
not only was his skin dark
but everything else about him
was strikingly dark and beautiful;
his dark-eyes, dark curly hair, dark brows
Oh wait! What about his heart?

At his very glimpse

The Labyrinth of My Life | Archita

I plugged out my earphones
and asked him the reason behind
him offering me his book
for we didn't even know each other
nor did I even ask him for it!

To my question, he reacted not;
nor did he respond,
instead kept the book next to me
with its upside turned down
and turned his face away looking
towards the darkest point from where the train
was to arrive in the next 15 minutes.

Curious at his conduct
and his strange constant gaze into the dark,
I asked him if he was to board
the same train which I had been waiting for.
He still remained silent, lost in his gaze
to which I better thought
to myself to remain shut.

Just when the train had arrived,
without any delay I thanked God,
grabbed the book from the bench,
thanked that *tall dark-handsome-unknown guy*,
bade him a good-bye
and got into my compartment.

After a minute stay on that platform,
where nobody boarded nor got down,
the train began to leave just when

I peeped through my window
to look for that man
who was to be found nowhere then.

Quite surprised at the thought
of his standing still on the platform
when I had already stepped onto the train,
I wondered where was he lost in the dark!

Lost in his thoughts,
I decided to have a glance at his gifted book
whose cover read the title
"Will you walk with the Shadow of my Death?"
The book without any author and publication details
sounded very strange and unfamiliar to me
and on opening its first page it read
"Until we meet the next time…"

By that time I came to know what his book
with the rest of its blank pages meant!
He was indeed lost forever
into the darkness of the dark hour.

www.ingramcontent.com/pod-product-compliance
Lightning Source LLC
Chambersburg PA
CBHW020445030426
42337CB00014B/1411